I0711538

HAND OF IRULEGI

Bakarne Atxukarro • Izaskun Zubialde
Asun Egurza

USAC Donostia-San Sebastián
(University Studies Abroad Consortium)

Translated by:

Bardner, Maximo

Franzoia, Kristina

Irujo Urdiroz, Xabier

Rodríguez, Giselle

Sangster, William

Welch, Ashleigh

Under the direction of:

Natalia Errazkin & Miriam Díaz

In a remote time, before a baby named Jesus was born, and before textbooks ever skope about Colombus or the French Revolution, let alone how to turn in digital homework, there was an eight-year-old boy named Olbap, who lived in the village of Irulegi.

There was a fort built high up in the mountains precisely so that it could not be reached by anyone with bad intentions.

The elders claimed it had been there for more than a thousand years.

Olbap did not actually live in the fort, but rather in a house on the hillside. Over time, the growing population left little room at the top of the mountain, so the village started expanding downwards.

There they built rectangular shaped houses similar to his, made out of mud and wood with a stone base. These structures housed the families, but they could also be used to keep the animals or store grain.

The houses were surrounded by vibrant and noisy day-to-day life: boys and girls behind every door, always ready to play; adults busy at their everyday chores; animals, voices, tools… All enclosed by a great-fortified wall that muted the noise and prevented entry without permission. Such was life in Irulegi.

And Olbap liked it that way. When he wasn't outside playing with his friends, he would spend hours in his dad's workshop. His dad was the local blacksmith and Olbap loved watching him make arrowheads, spears and daggers. His dad was so good that his name was well known even outside the village, which made people come from near and far to acquire the artifacts that Olbap found so fascinating.

In exchange, his dad received round pieces of metal called coins. With these coins, he could bring home more grain to make bread, wool for making clothes and fresh meat that Olbap's mom would cook with vegetables from the garden. His mom was a great cook; the food she made was delicious.

One day, Olbap decided to learn his father's trade. His dad was surprised because his son did not have the strength nor the skill to successfully hit an anvil or heat up the furnace. However, he finally gave in to his son's persistence and looked around his shop to give him something to start with.

"Take this metal and see what you can make of it! I am sure you will think of something."
He told him this handing him a thin sheet of bronze.

Olbap thanked him with surprise. He imagined he would start by pounding with the hammer, just as he had seen his father do. It did not even occur to him that he would have to come up with something to make from such a thing. What was it for?

He picked up a finely pointed metal awl. He thought that its sharp tip would allow him to draw something on the bronze sheet…but what?

Olbap raised his hands to his head to concentrate and covered his face, allowing the darkness to inspire him. The streaks of light peeking through his fingers gave him the inspiration he needed. "That's it! I'll draw my own hand!"

Without thinking twice, he placed his right hand on the sheet of metal and thought to trace the silhouette with the metal awl. Then, he realized his hand was too small and it would not turn out right. He needed a different model.

In that exact moment, his brother entered the workshop. At fourteen years old, between working in the shop with his father and in the fields with his mother, his brother had very little time to play. It was a stoke of luck to find him unoccupied.

Olbap thought his brother's hand could work as his model, but was not confident that his brother would spend what little free time he had helping him. In fact, he ran the risk of being scolded for even suggesting it. He did not want to give up before trying though, so he asked as nicely as he could:

"Would you mind helping me? I'm working on a project and I could use someone like you."

To his surprise, his brother stopped what he was doing and turned his attention to Olbap. Curiosity got the best of him.

"Me?" his brother asked, surprised.

"Yes, you! I promise it will be quick. Let me see your hand."

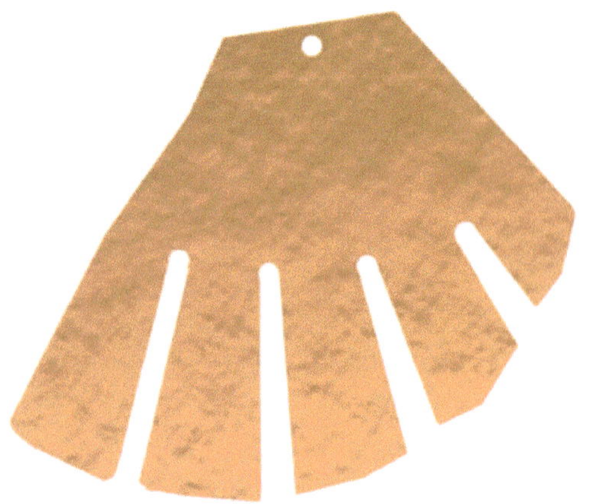

With this, Olbap got the results he was looking for. He was very proud of his work, but quickly started to realize his brother was growing impatient. Since he did not want to waste his brother´s time, he let him leave.

The truth is that Olbap wasn't even sure why he decided to trace a hand on the metal but he certainly enjoyed studying it over and over. He was so proud that he wanted to make sure it was perfect; therefore, he drew a nail on each finger. Olbap created a beautiful hand.

He even drew lines similar to those on his palm. In all certainty, drawing these lines on the metal made it appear more realistic.

Nevertheless, the hand was still missing something. Suddenly, he came up with something. Without thinking twice, Olbap ran to his dad as fast as possible.

"Could you please teach me how to write?"

"What? All of a sudden?"

"Yes."

"Listen son, writing is not something you can learn in a day. It takes time."

"I know, but if I watch you write I can learn."

"Okay, but you have to take into consideration that you will have to learn another language because the sounds of our language do not exist in the alphabet that I know. Therefore, some of those sounds cannot be written."

"Well, no worries, that's fine. I will invent my own way to write those sounds."

"Ha ha ha, if anyone could do so, it would be you. With your determination and imagination in that head of yours, no one can stop you."

Just like that, Olbap jumped right into a world that was unknown to him. He understood that things needed to have a name in order to exist. Therefore, he started by learning the words and symbols that could represent all he saw and felt. Some of them were harder than others, but all together it allowed Olbap to form his ideas in writing and transmit his thoughts at every moment.

His dad used a thin branch and blocks of fresh clay to draw the symbols that Olbap learned and reproduced repeatedly in the sand, dirt, or any surface he could find. Then, he taught him how to combine those signs in order to create meaningful phrases. It was perfect! Just what his bronze hand needed.

After some time, when he finally thought he was ready, he went back to his dad's shop to get the hand he made. With the awl, he began to mark the symbols he learned and started to form words. He marked a total of 40 symbols and 5 words.

Just as his father had warned him, he found it hard to pair some of the symbols with the sounds he wanted. This didn't stop Olbap, and just as he promised, he took the liberty of creating new symbols for these sounds; like the letter T.

He was so proud of the work he had done and thought that it would be a shame if it got lost. So, he decided to hang the hand on the front door of his house to welcome all visitors. Upon arrival, visitors would see an open and welcoming hand signaling friendship, instead of the closed fist that the elders were shown by their enemies.

Plus, the first word he had written was "Sorioneku" (fortunate). Who would reject or resent such a welcome?"

Olbap couldn't wait to tell his father about his magnificent idea and show him his masterpiece, so he ran to find him. However, he did not get the reaction he expected.

"You seriously wrote on bronze? Don't you know that people who actually write do so on lead? Also, what is this strange symbol, T? It doesn't mean anything. Is that something you made up? Do you think anyone will understand this? You have some nerve!"

Olbap felt so sad and disappointed. He thought that his father would appreciate his art and his effort to learn.

"Of course I appreciate it and I congratulate you for it. I'm sorry if I was harsh, but the war between the Sertorians and the Pompeians has me on edge."

Olbap did not really understand what his father was talking about. He had heard that there were groups from the Roman Empire fighting each other for power and were closing in on Irulegi. But they had no right to ruin his moment of glory. Who cares about the Romans?

Apparently, his father cared about the Romans and about war. That is why he had paid almost no attention to Olbap. What bad timing!

With this thought, he grabbed the hand and looked at it one more time. It was beautiful, perfect even. "I will hang it up on the door," he told himself. "But first I will shape it into a real hand."

Despite his sadness, he returned to the shop and trimmed the metal. This made him feel a little better. Regardless of the Romans and his dad's worry, his hand would still look great on his front door.

He walked up to the entrance of his house and nailed the hand to the door by the wrist. The five fingers remained pointing downwards with the words welcoming any newcomers.

With a smile on his face, he observed the shiny object. It might not have been lead, but to him it was even better.

All of a sudden, his dad screamed, "Run! We need to escape! The Romans set fire to Irulegi and if we do not get out, they will burn us to ashes!"

Left with no other choice, they rushed out of the village and did not look back. The hand was left there by itself, abandoned, sad and forgotten, hanging by a nail with no one there to admire it.

No one? More than 2,000 years later a group of archaeologists found the hand that Olbap left behind. By reading the first word, they concluded that the people in Irulegi were happy and wished good fortune upon all who visited. This society was capable of writing Sorioneku, the first textual word discovered in the Vasconic language, the ancestral language of the Basque language today.

Acknowledgment

The village of Irulegi (Navarre, Aranguren Valley) was inhabited between the middle of the Bronze Age (15th Century B.C. to the 11th Century B.C.) and the end of the Iron Age (1st Century B.C.). It burned to the ground during a war between two Roman factions, and its inhabitants had to abandon their homes and leave all behind.

More than two thousand years later on June 18, 2021, an excavation took place and a bronze hand was discovered. The find was made public on November 14 of the following year.

The most amazing part of the piece was the inscription that was found engraved on the hand: A total of five words, distributed in four lines, written in an Iberian alphabet but with unique properties such as the T symbol, which does not correspond to the original alphabet they used.

The transcription of the text to the Latin alphabet resulted in a word recognizable in the Basque language we know today: Sorioneku (one who has good fortune).

This was a very important discovery because it is the oldest Vasconic text found to this day and it demonstrates that Basque was spoken in Irulegi as early as the first century, B.C.

The discovery also demonstrates that those who could write, adapted the Latin alphabet they knew to transcribe the phonemes of the spoken Basque language. Furthermore, they introduced new, written symbols to express the Basque sounds that the Latin alphabet could not replicate.

Upon hearing about this discovery, we understood that it was important for it to be known by people of all ages, not just adults. We wanted this news to be appreciated by everyone, even the youngest of children.

This is how the story came to be. During its elaboration we depended on the close collaboration with archaeologist Teresa Lacosta Ramírez and the Aranzadi Science Society. Your help was indispensable for the writing of this story, and we are very grateful.

With their efforts and yours, all that is left is to enjoy and walk through history holding on to the Hand of Irulegi.

Other books by the authors

Basque Mythology: Stories for kids
Herensuge (English Edition)
Tartalo (English Edition)
Stories of Basque Mythology for Kids: A Compilation of
Classic Stories
Stories of Basque Mythology for Children
Without a Net. Her Story.
Olentzero and Mari Domingi
A mole in the garden
Lekim: The cave dwelling boy
DOG AND WOLF - BASQUE MYTHOLOGY FOR KIDS
(STORIES OF BASQUE MYTHOLOGY FOR KIDS - A
COMPILATION OF CLASSIC STORIES Book 1)
(English Edition)
Basajaun: The Lord of the Woods
MARI (English Edition)
Four Brothers (English Edition)
The Three Secrets (English Edition)
Atarrabi and Mikelats (English Edition)
The Hunchbacked Brothers (English Edition)